W9-APX-033

Great Moments in
Olympic
BASKETBALL

By Doug Williams

Great
Moments in
OLYMPIC
SPORTS

SportsZone
An Imprint of Abdo Publishing
www.abdopublishing.com

THE BRYANT LIBRARY
2 PAPER MILL ROAD
ROSLYN, NY 11576-2193

www.abdopublishing.com

Published by Abdo Publishing, a division of ABDO, PO Box 398166, Minneapolis, Minnesota 55439. Copyright © 2015 by Abdo Consulting Group, Inc. International copyrights reserved in all countries. No part of this book may be reproduced in any form without written permission from the publisher. SportsZone™ is a trademark and logo of Abdo Publishing.

Printed in the United States of America, North Mankato, Minnesota
042014
092014

THIS BOOK CONTAINS
RECYCLED MATERIALS

Cover Photo: Dusan Vranic/AP Images
Interior Photos: Dusan Vranic/AP Images, 1, 44, 46–47, 50; John Gaps III/AP Images, 6–7; Susan Ragan/AP Images, 8; AP Images, 12, 17, 19, 20–21, 26–27, 32, 34–35; Press Association/AP Images, 14–15; Bettmann/Corbis, 22, 25, 31; Pete Leabo/AP Images, 39; Michael Conroy/AP Images, 40–41; Charlie Riedel/AP Images, 52; Victor R. Caivano/AP Images, 54–55; Charles Krupa/AP Images, 59

Editor: Chrös McDougall
Series Designer: Craig Hinton

Library of Congress Control Number: 2014932870

Cataloging-in-Publication Data
Williams, Doug.
  Great moments in Olympic basketball / Doug Williams.
    p. cm. -- (Great moments in Olympic sports)
  Includes bibliographical references and index.
  ISBN 978-1-62403-393-3
  1. Basketball--Juvenile literature. 2. Olympics--Juvenile literature.   I. Title.
  796.323--dc23

                                                                    2014932870

Contents

Introduction

Basketball was invented in a Massachusetts gymnasium in 1891. The first of the modern Olympic Games took place four years later. However, it was not until 1936 that basketball was welcomed into the Games as a medal sport.

Basketball was a much different game in 1936 than it is today. For one thing, only men played in those Olympics in Berlin, Germany. The game also was much slower with lower scores. Also, Olympic basketball games were played outdoors then. But one thing has stayed the same over the years: US teams have dominated.

The US men have won 14 of 18 Olympic tournaments going into the 2016 Games. Women's basketball was added to the Olympics in 1976. US women's teams have won gold medals in seven of the 10 Olympic competitions.

The 1992 Olympics were the first in which National Basketball Association (NBA) players were allowed to participate. The NBA players only helped the US men dominate further. But the gap has closed in recent years. International participation in basketball skyrocketed after the 1992 Games. Great men's and women's players come from all over the world. These players have helped countries such as Australia, Argentina, Brazil, Italy, Lithuania, and Russia excel in the Olympics.

1

Barcelona 1992:
THE DREAM TEAM

Less than 10 minutes remained in the first half. Things were not going well for the US Olympic men's basketball team. Team USA was heavily favored coming into the gold-medal game of the 1992 Olympic Games in Barcelona, Spain. But Croatia had just gone on an 18–9 run and now led 25–23.

The US squad had easily won all seven of its previous Olympic games. Now suddenly the US "Dream Team" of NBA stars was trailing. The arena was filled with the

Team USA's Patrick Ewing grabs a rebound as teammate Scottie Pippen looks on during the 1992 Olympic gold-medal game against Croatia.

US forward Charles Barkley scores over Brazil's Israel Machado during a game at the 1992 Olympics in Barcelona, Spain.

cheers of European fans. They were eager to see an upset of a team that had seemed unbeatable.

One of Team USA's earlier Olympic wins had come against Croatia. The Dream Team cruised to a 33-point win. But in the championship game, Croatia came out with a slower style. Patiently, the Croatians worked for good shots. Croatia did not have superstars on the level of Team USA. But stars Toni Kukoc, Drazen Petrovic, and Dino Radja all played in the NBA. And in this game, they were making their shots.

Croatia took the 25–23 lead with approximately 9:42 left in the first half. That's when Team USA finally came to life. Forward Charles Barkley made a long three-point shot. That put Team USA up 26–25. Center David Robinson blocked Croatia's next shot. That led to an easy basket for Clyde Drexler. After a hard-fought defensive stop, Robinson scored on a tip-in dunk. Croatia got one basket. But then Chris Mullin followed that up with a three-pointer. Team USA now led 33–27.

Within minutes, the US lead was up to 18 points. The Croatian players continued to put up a noble effort. But they could not stick with the Dream Team. No one could. The Americans went on to win 117–85. The victory clinched the United States' first Olympic gold medal in men's basketball since 1984.

It was the crowning moment for the Dream Team. The 1992 Olympics were the first to include NBA players. The Dream Team, composed of 11 of the NBA's greatest players and college star Christian Laettner, was perhaps the finest ever assembled. It had Michael Jordan, Earvin "Magic" Johnson, Drexler, and John Stockton as guards. Patrick Ewing and Robinson were its centers. And Larry Bird, Barkley, Karl Malone, Mullin, Scottie Pippen, and Laettner were forwards. All except Laettner would later be elected to the Naismith Memorial Basketball Hall of Fame.

The Dream Team won its games by an average of 43.8 points per game. Croatia's 32–point loss in the final was the Dream Team's smallest margin of victory.

Popular Americans

Throughout the 1992 Olympics, crowds followed the US superstars wherever they went. The NBA had seen a great rise in popularity during the 1980s. That led to an increase in global television coverage. Players such as Jordan, Bird, and Johnson were heroes even to their Olympic opponents. Several players on opposing Olympic teams asked US players for autographs or pictures before games.

Lithuania's Moment in Bronze

The Lithuanian men's team was a fan favorite in Barcelona at the 1992 Olympics. Not only was it talented, but its players also wore bright, tie-dyed uniforms in the national colors. The uniforms were a tribute to the US rock band the Grateful Dead, which helped fund the team. Lithuania lost to Team USA in the semifinals. In the bronze-medal game, Lithuania beat a team composed of players from the former Soviet Union 82–78. The Soviets had re-occupied Lithuania in 1944. So the victory was sweet for the newly independent nation. Said Lithuanian star Sarunas Marciulionis: "I know how people will react in Lithuania. It's a holiday now."

"It was like Elvis and the Beatles put together," Team USA coach Chuck Daly said of the experience. "Traveling with the Dream Team was like traveling with 12 rock stars. That's all I can compare it to."

Yet these rock stars of basketball were on a mission. Four years earlier, the 1988 Olympics in Seoul, South Korea, had ended in disappointment. The US squad was composed of college stars. Many still favored the United States to win gold. However, Team USA lost to the Soviet Union in the semifinals. A win over Australia to claim the bronze medal did little to ease the bitter feeling.

In 1989, the rules changed to allow for NBA players in the 1992 Summer Games. The top American basketball players were eager for redemption. USA Basketball officials selected the team over several

The Dream Team members stand on the podium with their gold medals after beating Croatia in the 1992 Olympic gold-medal game.

months in 1991 and 1992. The best of the best players signed up to play for Team USA. The legendary squad took on the Dream Team nickname.

The Dream Team made its debut against Cuba in the Tournament of the Americas in June 1992. The result was a lopsided 136–57 win. The Cuban basketball coach said the Americans were unstoppable. The US squad won its six games in that tournament by an average of 51.5 points. The tournament championship qualified Team USA for the 1992 Olympics.

The Dream Team was an overwhelming favorite when it arrived at the Olympics in Barcelona. The Americans opened with a 116–48 victory over the African nation of Angola. They then defeated Croatia, Germany, Brazil, Spain, and Puerto Rico to reach the semifinals against Lithuania. Lithuania was a strong team. It had four players who had played for the Soviet team that beat Team USA in 1988. In this game, however, the Americans beat Lithuania 127–76.

That set up the championship game against Croatia. Jordan scored 22 points to lead the United States to its convincing victory.

"I don't think there will ever be a better team," the Chicago Bulls' star said after the game.

Eighteen years later, the Dream Team was elected as a unit to the National Basketball Hall of Fame. But to those who saw Team USA play in 1992, there was no need to wait that long. Its greatness was apparent.

"They knew they were playing the best in the world," Daly said of Team USA's opponents. "They'll go home and for the rest of their lives be able to tell their kids, 'I played against Michael Jordan and Magic Johnson and Larry Bird.' "

2

Berlin 1936:
BASKETBALL'S OLYMPIC DEBUT

Dr. James Naismith had invented basketball in 1891 in Springfield, Massachusetts. That was five years before the first modern Olympic Games. After spreading across the globe, basketball was finally added to the Games in 1936. The Olympics that year were held in Berlin, Germany. But the sport at those 1936 Games was very different from how it is today. There was no three-point line. Players rarely dunked. Scores were also much lower than in today's games.

The Philippines and Mexico play in the second round of the basketball tournament at the 1936 Olympic Games in Berlin, Germany.

Twenty-two nations committed to send teams. Naismith, 74, was invited to the Olympics and honored as the sport's founder.

Unexpected Rules

The US team was selected from the best players from the two top amateur teams at a qualifying tournament in New York, plus one college player. Team USA sailed across the Atlantic to get to Berlin. But when it arrived, it received a surprise. Several rules for the Olympics had been set without US input. One allowed just seven players for any team to suit up for a contest. That meant US coach James Needles was forced to leave half of his team in the stands for each game. Also, it had been decided that the games would be played outdoors. The courts were composed of hard-packed clay and sand. Another rule said that all players taller than 6 feet 2 inches be banned. However, it was overturned after US officials complained.

The Americans were still in for another surprise. The basketballs provided were much different than the ones used in the United States. The balls were smaller, lighter, and not suited for outside games.

"It wasn't heavy like a regular basketball," said Francis Johnson, a member of the US team in 1936. "You would shoot it and the wind might catch it and blow it three or four feet to the side."

Athletes show off Team USA uniforms for the 1936 Olympics.
They are, *from left*, basketball, track, sailing, and boxing.

The Americans were supposed to play Spain in their opener. But the Spanish team never showed up because of the civil war back home. Team USA was awarded a victory by forfeit. It would be the first of 63 consecutive Olympic victories by the US men.

Following the forfeit over Spain, the United States easily beat Estonia, the Philippines, and Mexico. That set up a game for the gold medal against Canada. Unfortunately for both teams, it rained before and during the game. The court turned into a muddy mess. Players found it almost impossible to dribble the ball.

"A dribble was not a dribble," said US guard Sam Balter, a former University of California, Los Angeles (UCLA) player. "It was a splash."

Team USA took a 15–4 lead at halftime. Through a hard rain in the second half, it won 19–8 to finish the tournament 5–0.

War Was Coming

What was most memorable about those Olympics for many of the US players was the atmosphere in Berlin. US captain Bill Wheatley recalled years later that the Nazi presence made it obvious Germany was preparing for war. Three years later, the Germans invaded Poland to start World War II.

A Glimpse of the Game

Basketball was played at the 1904 Olympic Games in St. Louis, Missouri, as a demonstration sport. Only three US college teams participated. Hiram College of Ohio defeated Latter-Day Saints University (now Brigham Young University) 25–18 for the championship.

German Nazi soldiers line up in attention with Nazi flags hanging in the background at the Opening Ceremony for the 1936 Olympics.

"There was no way you could get away from the Hitler influence," Wheatley said of German Chancellor Adolf Hitler. "Every morning he used to march 1,000 of his flashiest-dressed troops past the Olympic Village in a kind of show of strength. Anyone with an ounce of brains could tell that there was a man and a country getting ready to make war."

Rome 1960:
ROMAN CONQUEST

The 1960 Olympic Games rank as one of the most memorable ever. First, there was the beauty and history of the host city—Rome, Italy. Second, many of the athletic performances were extraordinary.

Ethiopia's Abebe Bikila ran barefoot to win the marathon. US sprinter Wilma Rudolph won three gold medals in track and field. Rafer Johnson won a duel with his good friend C. K. Yang of Taiwan to take the decathlon. Boxer Cassius Clay of Kentucky won gold.

Jerry Lucas of Ohio State University was one of several college stars who made up the 1960 US Olympic squad that played in Rome, Italy.

Team USA's Jerry Lucas (11) puts up a shot against Italy during the 1960 Olympic Games.

He would later change his name to Muhammad Ali and be known across the world.

And on the basketball court, the United States had perhaps the greatest men's team ever seen to that point. Team USA swept aside all comers. The Americans played eight games. They won all eight and beat opponents by an average of 42.4 points.

The US players were mostly college players. Jerry West led the University of West Virginia. Oscar Robertson was a star at the University of Cincinnati. Jerry Lucas played at Ohio State University. Ten of the 12 US players later went on to play in the NBA. Four players made it to the Hall of Fame. Coach Pete Newell became a Hall of Famer as well. West called it "the greatest amateur team that ever played."

One rule had been changed since the previous Olympics. The 1956 Games had been held in Melbourne, Australia. Led by center Bill Russell, Team USA had easily won the gold medal. Officials wanted to lessen the impact of the tallest players, such as Russell. So a wider key under the basket was adopted for the 1960 Olympics. Centers could only stay in the lane for three seconds. The rule was supposed to keep centers farther from the hoop. It had little, if any, impact.

In 1960, the Americans opened with an 88–54 victory over host Italy. Team USA then scored more than 100 points per game in victories over Japan, Hungary, Yugoslavia, and Uruguay. The Americans' next opponent proved much tougher.

The Biggest Challenge

The Soviet Union was 4–1. It featured a powerful center in Janis Krumins. He was 7 feet 2 inches and weighed 311 pounds. At halftime, Team USA led just 35–28. That's when Newell turned up the pressure on its foe.

"Pete said in the locker room, 'They think they can beat us. Let's change their minds,' " said US player Darrall Imhoff, a 6-foot-11 center from the University of California. "We put on a full-court press."

South American Power

Basketball was introduced to Brazil just a few years after the sport was invented in 1891. That early introduction helped Brazil become one of the early powers in the sport. Brazil won the Olympic bronze medal in 1960. It also claimed bronze medals at the 1948 Games in London, England, and the 1964 Games in Tokyo, Japan. Wlamir Marques was the star of the 1960 team. He averaged 18.3 points per game. Marques scored 19 points to lead his team against Team USA. He also played on Brazil's 1956, 1964, and 1968 Olympic teams. Marques later was elected to the International Basketball Federation Hall of Fame.

The pressure defense forced the Soviets to make mistakes. The Americans scored 20 points in the first five minutes of the second half. They went on to win easily 81–57. West led Team USA with 19 points.

Team USA then defeated Italy again. Finally, the US squad beat Brazil in their final game to secure the gold medal. Lucas scored 25 points in the 90–63 win over Brazil. The victory extended the Americans' all-time Olympic basketball record to 36–0.

Robertson and Lucas led a very balanced US team. Both averaged around 17 points per game. West, Terry Dischinger, and Adrian Smith also averaged more than 10 points per game. Robertson said the team had no weaknesses.

"We had speed, quickness, and stamina, played stifling defense, and rebounded at both ends of the court," Robertson said. "We averaged 102 points and held our opponents to fewer than 60. We played textbook

US basketball players Jerry West, *middle left*, and Oscar Robertson, *middle right*, celebrate on the podium after winning the 1960 Olympic gold medal.

basketball, blocking out under the boards, setting picks for each other, moving without the ball to get open for good shots. Everyone played his role."

The 1960 US men's basketball team might not have been as famous as the 1992 Dream Team. But the two teams did share one distinction. Both teams were inducted into the Naismith Memorial Hall of Fame.

Munich 1972:
A SHOCKING UPSET

In 1972, it seemed impossible that the United States wouldn't win the Olympic gold medal in men's basketball. Team USA had never lost in 55 Olympic contests. It had won all seven gold medals since 1936.

The 1972 Games were in Munich, West Germany. The United States again sent some of the nation's best college players. Tommy Burleson was a 7-foot-4 center from North Carolina State University. Tom McMillen was a 6-foot-11 forward from the University of Maryland. That duo made the US strong under the basket. The team also

Team USA, shown in a game against Cuba, came into the 1972 Olympic Games in Munich, West Germany, as a favorite to win an eighth straight Olympic basketball gold medal.

had proven scorers at guard. Among them were Doug Collins of Illinois State University, Kevin Joyce of the University of South Carolina, and Ed Ratleff of Long Beach State University. Plus, coach Henry Iba had Olympic experience. He twice had led US teams to Olympic golds.

But the 1972 Olympic basketball tournament was about to make history. It would produce one of the most controversial upsets in sports.

Setting the Stage

The Americans opened with a 66–35 win over Czechoslovakia. Two more easy wins followed over Australia and Cuba. Team USA struggled with Brazil, but won 61–54. Then came easy victories over Egypt, Spain, Japan, and Italy. That put the Americans in the gold-medal game.

Team USA would face the Soviet Union. Both teams were 8–0. The Soviets had been almost as dominating as the Americans. Team USA had won games by an average margin of 32.5 points. The Soviets had won games by an average of 20.75 points. Since the 1952 Olympics, the Soviet Union had been a basketball power second only to Team USA. It won the bronze medal at the previous Games, in 1968. However, the Soviet Union had won four consecutive silver medals from 1952 to 1964.

The Soviet Union had a deep, experienced team. Most of the players had been together for several years. They were led by 6-foot-3 guard

Growth of Women's Basketball

The 1972 Olympics was the last Games without a women's basketball tournament. Yet 1972 proved to be important. That year, a US federal law called Title IX was passed. It required that schools receiving federal funds must provide equal opportunities for men and women. That included athletics. Title IX sparked a growth in women's basketball programs in US high schools and colleges. It paved the way for future success. Women made their basketball debut at the 1976 Olympics in Montreal, Canada.

Sergei Belov and 6-foot-7 forward Aleksandr Belov. The team had proven how good it was by winning eight of nine games on a US tour in 1971.

The American players, selected earlier that year, had played just a handful of games together. It was the tallest US team ever selected. Nine players stood taller than 6 feet 6 inches. But it also was the youngest team. Nine of the 12 players were 20 or 21 years old.

A Controversial Conclusion

The Soviets took a quick 7–0 lead to start the gold-medal game. They held a 26–21 lead at halftime. But the Americans kept narrowing the gap. Finally, with 40 seconds remaining in the game, Team USA climbed to within a point. It trailed just 49–48.

The Soviets then passed the ball around. That took 30 seconds off the clock. Only 10 seconds remained. Then Team USA's Collins intercepted a pass by Aleksandr Belov. Collins dribbled the length of court and went up for a layup. Three seconds remained as he took the shot. However, a defender crashed into Collins. The layup missed. Collins fell hard to the court and was knocked unconscious. Officials called a foul.

Collins regained consciousness after approximately 10 seconds. He soon found himself at the free-throw line for two shots. He made the first to tie the game 49–49. As he was shooting the second, a buzzer sounded. Collins shot anyway. It was good. The shot gave Team USA a 50–49 lead.

The Soviets quickly inbounded the ball and tried to get it upcourt. One second remained on the clock. Then the officials stopped the game. They ruled the Soviet coach had tried to call a timeout between Collins's free throws. They said he had pushed a button connected to the buzzer to signal the referees. But the buzzer had been ignored. The chief of officials ruled the Soviets should again inbound the ball with three seconds left.

The Soviets threw the ball in. This time they were only able to put up a long shot. It didn't come close. The horn sounded, signaling the end of the game. US players celebrated what they thought was their victory. Some even left the court.

The US players celebrate what they believed to be an Olympic gold medal at the 1972 Olympics. Referees soon called the players back to the court to replay the ending.

Moments later, however, officials ordered players back. They were told to replay the final three seconds for a third time. The officials said the clock had not been properly reset to show three seconds remained.

"We couldn't believe that they were giving them all these chances," US forward Mike Bantom said. "It was like they were going to let them do it until they got it right."

The Soviet Union's Aleksandr Belov scores the winning basket against Team USA in the 1972 Olympic gold-medal game.

The Soviets quickly got the ball in. Ivan Edeshko threw a full-court pass to Aleksandr Belov near the US basket. Belov went up over two US players to catch the ball. Then he laid the ball into the basket. The horn sounded. This time the Soviets had a 51–50 victory. The Americans were stunned. They believed they'd been robbed. Meanwhile, the Soviets celebrated wildly.

US officials appealed the decision to the International Basketball Federation. The appeal was rejected. The Soviet victory stood. American players were so angry they declined to accept their silver medals. Collins said the feeling of having a victory taken away was devastating.

"It was sort of like being on top of the Sears Tower in Chicago celebrating, and then being thrown off and falling 100 floors to the ground," he said. "That's the kind of emptiness and sick feeling I felt."

Finally, the US streak of perfection in the Olympics was over. After 63 straight victories came one bitter defeat. More than 40 years later, the US players still had not accepted their silver medals.

"If we had gotten beat, I would be proud to display my silver medal today," said Bantom years later. "But we didn't get beat. We got cheated."

Los Angeles 1984:
BASKETBALL QUEENS

The buzzer sounded to end the 1984 Olympic women's gold-medal basketball game. The US players went wild. They jumped and hugged and celebrated all over the court. Finally, they had Team USA's first Olympic gold in women's basketball. And they had done it on home soil in Los Angeles, California.

Team USA had just completed an 85–55 victory over South Korea. US star Cheryl Miller led the charge. She scored 16 points and pulled down 11 rebounds.

Team USA's Lynette Woodard goes up for a shot against South Korea during the 1984 Olympic Games in Los Angeles, California.

The South Koreans had rallied to come within 10 points early in the second half. But Miller and her teammates countered. They outscored their opponents 14–0 over the next few minutes to pull away and secure the victory. Now, with the game over, the US players picked up coach Pat Summitt. They carried her around the floor in triumph. It was a moment to savor.

Women's basketball was first introduced to the Olympics in 1976. The United States was no match for the Soviet Union then. Team USA had to settle for the silver medal. Four years later, the chance for a gold was lost. The United States boycotted those games in Moscow, Soviet Union. The boycott was to protest the Soviet invasion of Afghanistan. Now, at long last, the US women were on top of the basketball world.

Summitt had been a player on the 1976 US Olympic team. Then she was an assistant coach on the 1980 team. She had been a part of the US program for eight years. "I know I was proud as a player," she said after the 1984 gold-medal game. "And as a coach, I'm just as proud."

The 1984 US roster had 12 players. Four of those players had been on the 1980 team. They were Denise Curry, Anne Donovan, Cindy Noble, and Lynette Woodard. For them, the victory was especially sweet. But even new US stars said they had never experienced such a feeling.

The Last Amateur Champions

The US men's team in 1984 was considered the strongest since 1960. Indiana University's Bobby Knight coached the squad. The team included such future NBA stars as Michael Jordan, Patrick Ewing, and Chris Mullin. All three were college stars at the time. Team USA went 8–0 and beat Spain 96–65 for the gold medal. It would be the last US team of college players to win gold.

"Right now, I've achieved my ultimate goal," Miller said. Added Janice Lawrence, who was part of two college national championship teams at Louisiana Tech University, "That was college. This is the world."

This Time, no Soviet Union

The United States had won a silver medal at the World Championships in 1983. It is the biggest international tournament outside the Olympics. That group, also coached by Summitt, lost to the Soviet Union 84–82 in the title game. Many US players returned for the 1984 Olympics.

There would be no Team USA-Soviet Union rematch at the 1984 Games, however. This time, the Soviets boycotted. They cited security concerns in a "hostile environment" as their reason. However, many believed the boycott was payback for the US boycott in 1980. Whatever the reason, US players were disappointed they didn't have a chance to play the two-time Olympic champions. "Now I'll always question who would have won," Miller said.

Yet the US team was filled with college stars. Miller and Pam McGee played for the University of Southern California (USC). Curry played at nearby UCLA. Meanwhile, Woodard starred at the University of Kansas and Donovan at Old Dominion University.

Team USA opened with an 83–55 victory over Yugoslavia. Miller scored 23 points in the win. Then came an 81–47 victory over Australia. An 84–47 decision over South Korea followed. The Americans raised their record to 4–0 with a 91–55 win over China. Team USA then earned a spot in the gold-medal game with a 92–61 victory over Canada. Donovan's 14 points led her team.

The gold-medal game rematch with the South Koreans began as a tight game. After six minutes, the score was 12–12. But Team USA then outscored its opponent 16–2. In the second half, the United States had another big run to ensure the victory.

The long-awaited first US Olympic championship was the result of a terrific team effort in the final. Every player scored. And in going 6–0, Team USA outscored its foes by an average of 32.7 points per game.

Summitt, who had a legendary career as coach of the women's team at the University of Tennessee, had been selected as the coach long in advance of the Games. She picked the team and coached it, emphasizing

US players celebrate their 1984 Olympic gold medal by carrying coach Pat Summitt around the court.

defense. She felt the pressure of trying to win the first Olympic championship. The victory meant she could finally relax.

"That job aged me years," Summitt said later. "I've never had anything stress me like that. For 2.5 years, not a day went by that I didn't think about the Olympics. . . . We couldn't have asked for better talent. It was an all-star collection. My main job was not to overcoach and to get those young women to play together."

At the 1988 Olympics in Seoul, South Korea, the US women finally had their chance to play the Soviet Union in the Olympics. This time, Team USA dominated in a 102–88 semifinal win.

6

Athens 2004:
THE WORLD'S GAME

The United States was unbeatable with amateur players in the Olympics from 1936 until 1972. Professional US men's players were just as dominant. They won gold medals in 1992, 1996, and 2000, going 24–0.

The 2004 Olympics returned to Greece. That is where the ancient Olympics were held. The modern Olympics returned in 1896 in that country as well. At the 2004 Games in Athens, basketball teams from around the

Italy's Giacomo Galanda reacts during the gold-medal game of the 2004 Olympic Games in Athens, Greece.

globe showed how far they had come. The 2004 Olympic tournament was arguably the most competitive one yet.

Team USA still stacked its roster with NBA stars. But the United States was no longer invincible. Basketball truly was a global game. And this time, the Games would not be golden for Team USA.

The US team in Athens was missing several NBA stars. Players such as Shaquille O'Neal, Kobe Bryant, Kevin Garnett, and Ray Allen decided not to play for Team USA for a variety of reasons. The absences left the team without any consistent three-point shooters. The team had just one proven point guard. It also wasn't considered a good passing team.

Still, coach Larry Brown's team was talented and the favorite. It had standouts such as Tim Duncan. The 6-foot-11 forward from the San Antonio Spurs had led his team to NBA titles in 1999 and 2003. Guards Allen Iverson of the Philadelphia 76ers and Dwyane Wade of the Miami Heat were great scorers. Nineteen-year-old star LeBron James of the Cleveland Cavaliers also was on the team.

But other countries had NBA stars, too. Argentina had Spurs guard Manu Ginobili. China had Houston Rockets center Yao Ming. Spain had Memphis Grizzlies forward Pau Gasol. Australia had center Andrew Bogut. Bogut became the first pick in the 2005 NBA Draft.

US Women Shine Again

While the US men struggled in Athens, the American women dominated. They defeated Australia 74–63 in the championship game. That gave them their third straight Olympic gold medal. The US women went 8–0 in Athens. Their average margin of victory was 23.8 points. Lisa Leslie, Dawn Staley, and Sheryl Swoopes all were part of their third Olympic championship team. Leslie led the US team by scoring 15.6 points per game. She also became Team USA's all-time Olympic scorer, rebounder, and shot blocker.

A Startling Start

Team USA came into the 2004 Olympics with a sterling record. It had played 111 total Olympic basketball games. Only two of those games ended in losses. A third loss came in the squad's opening game in 2004. Puerto Rico came out hot. It held a 22-point lead over Team USA at halftime. Puerto Rico went on to shock Team USA with a 92–73 win. It was the most lopsided loss in Olympic history for the US men.

The US team made only 35 percent of its shots. Only three of its 24 three-point shots were good. And it committed 22 turnovers. On the other hand, Puerto Rico made 56 percent of its shots. Carlos Arroyo, a guard for the Utah Jazz, led Puerto Rico with 24 points. Brown said Team USA was outplayed.

The Americans responded with a 77–71 victory over Greece. Then came an 89–79 victory over Australia. Duncan had 18 points and

Argentina's Fabricio Oberto and Luis Scola celebrate after beating Team USA in the semifinals of the 2004 Olympics.

11 rebounds in that win. In its fourth game, however, Team USA fell to Lithuania 94–90. The Lithuanians made 13 of 27 three-point shots. They also outscored Team USA 27–21 in the fourth quarter. The Americans had lost twice already in Athens. That equaled the total number of losses for the US men from 1936 to 2000.

Team USA rebounded with consecutive victories over Angola and Spain. That sent the squad to the tournament semifinals. It still had a chance at a gold medal. Argentina, however, squashed those hopes with an 89–81 victory.

Ginobili scored 29 points for Argentina, which again outshot the Americans. Team USA made just 42 percent of its shots. It made just three of its three-point shots. The Argentines made 11 three-pointers and shot 54 percent overall.

"The rest of the world is getting better and the States isn't bringing their best players," Ginobili said. Team USA's Iverson agreed. He said the days of American dominance weren't automatic anymore. "You can't just show up at a basketball game and feel that because you have USA across your chest you're going to win the game," he said.

Argentina advanced to the gold-medal game. It defeated Italy 84–69. The win made Argentina the first nation besides the United States or the Soviet Union to win gold. The United States met Lithuania for a rematch in the bronze-medal game. This time Team USA won 104–96. Shawn Marion led the US team with 22 points. Coming home with a bronze instead of a gold was disappointing. But after losing three games in Athens, the US players were happy to get any medal.

"We wanted gold," Marion said. "But I'm going to take anything right now. That's the way it is."

Beijing 2008:
THE REDEEM TEAM

If 1992 had been a dream for US Olympic men's basketball, 2004 was a nightmare. The US men had failed to reach the Olympic gold-medal game for only the second time. Forward Carmelo Anthony called the Athens experience "America's lowest point" in the sport. But American men's teams had fallen short elsewhere, too. The United States hadn't won a major international competition since the 2000 Olympics in Sydney, Australia. In 2002, it finished sixth in the World Championships.

Kobe Bryant and Team USA set out for redemption at the 2008 Olympic Games in Beijing, China.

USA Basketball is the national governing organization for the sport. Its most high-profile task is running the national teams. USA Basketball hired Jerry Colangelo in 2005 to lead the turnaround. The former NBA coach and executive set a new program in place. The goal was to find redemption at the 2008 Olympic Games in Beijing, China. As such, the players took on the nickname "The Redeem Team." The nickname was a play on the Dream Team nickname. But the goal was simple: redeem US basketball by winning a gold medal. The Redeem Team indeed took the United States back to the Olympic peak in 2008. But its foundation was built in 2005.

Colangelo's new program had several key features. First was commitment. Previous US Olympic teams had been put together in the months leading up to the Games. Under Colangelo, the top US players in 2005 had to commit to three years on the national team. Second, Duke University coach Mike Krzyzewski was hired to lead the US team. He would provide stability. Plus, his system embraced aspects of international basketball that often had been overlooked by US teams. The importance of three-point shooting was one element. Playing zone defense, as well as man-to-man defense, was another. Zone defense is limited in the NBA.

Many of the best US basketball players stepped up for the challenge. The final roster had 12 players. They had been together for at least two years before the Beijing Games. The core players had played 29 games together before Game 1 in China.

"From Athens we learned we need time to develop camaraderie," Krzyzewski said. "We have to be committed to one another before we can be committed to the team. We're developing a program, not selecting a team."

Team USA qualified for the Olympics through a tournament in 2007. The starting five from the qualifying tournament remained the starting five in Beijing. Jason Kidd was the point guard. Kobe Bryant played shooting guard. LeBron James and Carmelo Anthony were the forwards. Dwight Howard was the starting center.

Best Women's Team Ever

How dominating was the US women's team at the 2008 Olympics in Beijing? Well, they extended their Olympic winning streak to 33 games by going 8–0. And they won games by an average of 37.6 points. Team USA made 54 percent of its shots. It held opponents to just 34 percent shooting. Four-time Olympic champion Lisa Leslie was the star. The Americans beat Australia 92–65 in the final. "This is the best women's team ever, thus far," said forward Tamika Catchings. "Every single year we get better and better."

Team USA's LeBron James goes up for a dunk against China at the 2008 Olympics.

Rematches and Domination

The Americans opened the Olympics with an anticipated game against China. Basketball was growing rapidly in the host country. A big reason for that was 7-foot-6 center Yao Ming. He starred for the Houston Rockets in the NBA. The Chinese proved little threat to the Redeem Team, though. Team USA won 101–70. Then it beat Angola 97–76. The United States improved to 3–0 by defeating Greece 92–69. Forward Chris Bosh and Bryant each scored 18 points in the win.

Next up was Spain. The Spaniards had won the World Championships in 2006. But they were no match for Team USA. James had 18 points, eight assists, and five rebounds in a 119–82 win.

Team USA then beat Germany 106–57 and Australia 116–85. That set up a semifinal game against Argentina. The Argentines had beaten the Americans in the 2004 Olympic semifinal on their way to a gold medal. This time, the Americans dominated. Team USA took a 30–11 lead before winning 101–81. Anthony's 21 points led the United States.

The win put Team USA back in the gold-medal game. A rematch with Spain was next. The Spaniards had lost to Team USA by 37 points already. They put up a much better fight with a medal on the line.

The Spanish team featured NBA star Pau Gasol. His brother, Marc Gasol, and Spain guard Rudy Fernandez, would join the NBA that fall. Together they helped Spain stay right with Team USA in a high-scoring duel. The game remained close to the end. Spain trailed just 104–99 with approximately 3.5 minutes left. Then redemption was sealed. Bryant scored four points. Guard Dwyane Wade added a three-pointer. It was his fourth of the game. The run helped Team USA pull away to a 118–107

The US men's basketball team stands on the podium as champions as the national anthem plays at the 2008 Olympics.

win. Krzyzewski later called it "one of the great games in international basketball history."

Team USA had indeed redeemed American basketball. The Americans went 8–0. They beat opponents by an average of 27.9 points. It marked the thirteenth gold medal for the US men in 17 Olympics.

As the game ended, US players celebrated. Kidd and Krzyzewski hugged. James and Anthony led the crowd in cheers of "USA! USA!" The US team was a collection of many of the best players in the world. For most of the year, they were fierce rivals in the NBA. But on this night, they stood with their arms around one another on the medal podium. They smiled, posed for pictures, and hung their medals around the neck of Krzyzewski.

For Anthony, it was a sweet counter to what had been a sour feeling in 2004. "I think we [put] American basketball back where it's supposed to be, which is at the top of the world," he said.

8

London 2012:
FIVE STRAIGHT

A little more than six minutes remained in the first half. Australia and the United States were tied 32–32. It was a semifinal game of the women's basketball tournament at the 2012 Olympic Games in London, England. The heavily favored Americans just couldn't pull away.

Team USA had crushed its first six straight opponents in London. The Americans had extended their Olympic

Team USA's Angel McCoughtry sails to the basket to score against Australia in the 2012 Olympic semifinals in London, England.

winning streak to 39 games. A fifth straight Olympic gold medal had seemed certain. Yet the Aussies weren't cooperating.

In less than a minute, the Australians took control. First, Samantha Richards made a long three-point shot. Then two straight US missed shots led to quick baskets for Australia's Suzy Batkovic and Rachel Jarry. Suddenly, Team USA trailed 39–32.

By halftime, Australia had a 47–43 lead. For the first time in 12 years, the Americans were behind at the half of an Olympic game. The Australians had made 61 percent of their shots. The team's 6-foot-8 star, Liz Cambage, had been unstoppable. She had 19 points. The Americans weren't discouraged, though. The veteran team actually was confident.

"We took what I think you could probably call Australia's best shot, [and] we were only down four," said US guard Sue Bird. "We took that as a positive. Obviously, we weren't happy. But we weren't concerned. Nobody had their head hanging low or anything like that."

The American women turned up the defensive pressure in the second half. They forced the Australians into some bad shots and turnovers. Then Team USA went on a run. It outscored Australia 10–3 to end the third quarter. In the fourth quarter, the Americans outscored Australia 21–14. Team USA went on to win 86–73.

The Australian Women

The US women have been dominant in recent Olympic Games. Other countries have been consistently good, too. The best after Team USA has been Australia. The Australians won a silver or bronze medal in every Games from 1996 to 2012. The Opals, as they are known in Australia, have five total medals. That ranks second all-time behind the United States. Australians such as Lauren Jackson and Liz Cambage became international stars. In 2012, Cambage dunked in a win over Russia. It was believed to be the first dunk ever in an Olympic women's game.

"We came out in the second half and once we got control of the game, it took off from there," said US coach Geno Auriemma.

The Streak Continues

The victory sent Team USA to the gold-medal game against France. The French had defeated Russia 81–64 in their semifinal. They were 7–0 in the tournament. However, they proved to be no match for the Americans.

Team USA jumped out to a 20–15 lead in the first quarter. The Americans rolled to an 86–50 victory. The US defense forced France into 21 turnovers. It also made the French players work for all of their shots. France made only 28 percent of its shots. All 12 players on the US team scored. Candace Parker's 21 points and 11 rebounds led the way.

The win extended the Americans' sterling Olympic streak. They had now won 41 consecutive Olympic games. Those wins included

Americans Win Rematch

The 2012 Olympic men's gold-medal game was a rematch from 2008. Again, the United States beat Spain. But Team USA's 107–100 win wasn't easy. The outcome was in doubt for most of the game. The contest featured 16 lead changes. Kevin Durant's 30 points helped Team USA hang on. The win meant the Americans went 8–0 for a second straight Olympics. The gold medal was their fifth in the past six Olympics. Five players averaged 10 points or more for a deep US team. Durant, of the NBA's Oklahoma City Thunder, averaged 19.5 points to lead US scorers.

five straight Olympic gold medals. The last time Team USA missed a gold medal was in 1992. That year, the squad won a bronze medal at the Games in Barcelona, Spain. The 2012 US team proved particularly dominant, though. The 36-point win was the largest margin of victory ever in a women's gold-medal game.

Women's basketball had seen steady growth in the United States during the streak of five gold medals. The college game grew bigger and more sophisticated than ever. Meanwhile, the Women's National Basketball Association (WNBA) began play in 1997. A steady flow of talented players continued to emerge from college and the WNBA. US tri-captains Bird, Diana Taurasi, and Tamika Catchings each won their third Olympic gold medal in 2012. Parker, Seimone Augustus, and Sylvia Fowles each won their second gold medal.

The US men's team has consistently won. But the US women actually have been more dominant. They lost just one international game

The US players celebrate in 2012 after winning the country's fifth straight Olympic gold medal in women's basketball.

from 1996 through 2012. That loss was in the semifinals of the 2006 World Championships.

"It just shows the depth and talent in our country," Taurasi said. "Women's basketball, it's our sport. It's our sport. We grew up playing since we were little and give it every single little bit of energy we have."

Auriemma said the women's triumph in London was just part of a long string of success. "The United States has had great teams since 1996 and we are just another one on the list," he said. "We accomplished the same thing they did and I don't know if that separates us. I think it just makes us equal."

Great
Olympians

Teresa Edwards (USA)
The guard was a key player on a record five US women's Olympic teams from 1984 through 2000. Those teams won four gold medals and one bronze.

Andrew Gaze (Australia)
He played in five Olympics from 1984 to 2000 and ranks as the number two all-time Olympic scorer.

Lauren Jackson (Australia)
The 6-foot-6 forward helped Australia win silver medals at the 2000, 2004, and 2008 Olympics, and a bronze medal in 2012.

LeBron James (USA)
The three-time Olympian (2004, 2008, and 2012) holds the US Olympic record for points (273) and assists (88).

Michael Jordan (USA)
A star for US gold-medal teams in 1984 and 1992, Jordan also holds US Olympic records for most field goals made (111) and attempted (223).

Lisa Leslie (USA)
The four-time gold medalist (1996, 2000, 2004, and 2008) is Team USA's all-time leader in points (488), rebounds (241), and blocked shots (36). She is tied with Teresa Edwards for most games played (32).

Cheryl Miller (USA)
Though she only played in one Olympics, in 1984, she led the Americans to their first gold medal. She led Team USA in scoring, rebounding, assists, and steals, and made an amazing 66 percent of her shots.

David Robinson (USA)
The 7-foot-1 center played in the 1988, 1992, and 1996 Olympics for Team USA. He has the record for most rebounds (124) and blocked shots (34).

Oscar Schmidt (Brazil)
He is the all-time leading scorer in Olympic history with 1,093 points. He played in five Olympics from 1980 to 1996 and was the leading scorer of the Games three times.

Glossary

AMATEUR
Players who are not paid.

ASSIST
A pass that leads directly to a basket.

BLOCK
A play in which a shooter's field goal attempt is knocked down by a defender before it can reach the rim.

BOYCOTT
In the Olympics, this describes the actions of certain nations that have decided not to send athletes to the Games, usually because of political reasons.

DEFENSE
The act of trying to stop an opponent from scoring a basket.

KEY
The area under the basket. It is usually designated by a different color on the floor of the court. The key in international basketball is a trapezoid shape as opposed to the rectangle shape more common in the United States.

REBOUND
A missed shot that is caught by a player.

VETERAN
A player with a lot of experience.

ZONE DEFENSE
In Olympic basketball, teams can play this type of defense in which players are responsible for guarding a certain area rather than one player. Zones are allowed in Olympic, college, and high school basketball. However, zone defense was long banned in the NBA.

For More Information

SELECTED BIBLIOGRAPHY

Amdur, Neil. "The Three Seconds That Never Seem to Run Out." *New York Times*. The New York Times Co., 28 July 2012. Web. 24 Feb. 2013.

Anderson, Kelli. "US shows depth in second half as they hand Australia crushing loss." *Sports Illustrated*. Time Warner, 9 Aug. 2012. Web. 24 Feb. 2013.

Araton, Harvey. "Theme Comes True: The Dream Team Captures the Gold." *New York Times*. The New York Times Co., 9 Aug. 1992. Web. 24 Feb. 2013.

Elderkin, Phil. "Talented US women's basketball team in drive toward gold medal." *The Christian Science Monitor*. Christian Science Publishing Co., 6 Aug. 1984. Web. 24 Feb. 2013.

Herzog, Brad. "The Dream Team of 1936." *Sports Illustrated*. Time Warner, 22 July 1996. Web. 24 Feb. 2013.

FURTHER READINGS

Cunningham, Carson. *American Hoops: US Men's Olympic Basketball from Berlin to Beijing*. Lincoln, NE: University of Nebraska Press, 2010.

Hughes, Rich. *Netting Out Basketball 1936: The Remarkable Story of the McPherson Refiners, the First Team to Dunk, Zone Press, and Win the Olympic Gold Medal*. Victoria, BC: Friesen Press, 2011.

Leslie, Lisa, with Larry Burnett. *Don't Let the Lipstick Fool You: The Making of a Champion*. New York: Kensington Publishing Corp., 2008.

McCallum, Jack. *Dream Team: How Michael, Magic, Larry, Charles and the Greatest Team of All Time Conquered the World and Changed the Game of Basketball Forever*. New York: Ballantine Books, 2012.

WEBSITES

To learn more about Great Moments in Olympic Sports, visit **booklinks.abdopublishing.com**. These links are routinely monitored and updated to provide the most current information available.

PLACES TO VISIT

Naismith Memorial Basketball Hall of Fame
1000 Hall of Fame Ave.
Springfield, MA, 01105
(877) 446-6752
www.hoophall.com
This basketball museum, founded in 1959, is located in the city where Dr. James Naismith invented the sport in 1891 at a YMCA. The hall's exhibit space includes displays and information for about 300 men and women from the United States and around the world who have played important roles in the game.

Women's Basketball Hall of Fame
700 Hall of Fame Drive
Knoxville, TN, 37915
(865) 633-9000
www.wbhof.com
Opened in 1999, this museum honors players, coaches, teams, and contributors to all levels of the women's game. More than 130 people have been inducted. Its mission statement is, "Honor the past, celebrate the present, and promote the future" of women's basketball.

Index

ABOUT THE AUTHOR

Doug Williams is a freelance writer and former newspaper editor. He covered three Olympics, in Los Angeles, California; Sydney, Australia; and Athens, Greece. This is his fourth book. He also writes about sports, travel, people, and pets for websites, newspapers, and magazines. He lives in San Diego, California, with his wife and enjoys hiking, cooking, reading, and spending time with his family.